A
LIFE'S
JOURNEY

REFLECTIONS
OF LIFE AND LOVE
THROUGH POETRY

BY BOBBY LATHAN JR.

WITH CONTRIBUTIONS
BY JOSÉ A. DUARTE AND MICHAEL JILBERT

PAPERBACK FIRST EDITION

Published by: Bobby R. Lathan Jr.
Email: bobby.lathan.the.author@gmail.com
Website: http://stores.lulu.com/bobbylathanjr
MySpace: http://www.myspace.com/bobbylathanjr

Editors and Proofreaders:
Nidia Alvarado
Tony Alvarez
Leticia Blanton
José A. Duarte
Bobby R. Lathan Jr.
Bobby R. Lathan Sr.
Shirley M. Lathan
Stephanie Lopez
Sonia Morales
Mayra Rojas
James P. Williams Jr.

ISBN: 978-0-578-00731-1
Library of Congress Control Number: 2009900627

To my parents
who are my loyal supporters
and
my future wife
I don't know whom you are
but I will find you someday

TABLE OF CONTENTS

TABLE OF CONTENTS (CONTINUED)

Photograph taken by
Bobby Lathan Sr., 1972
Maternal grandparents' house
Alexandria, LA

Yeah, believe it or not, it's me as an infant.

ACKNOWLEDGMENTS

First and foremost I would like to thank GOD and Jesus Christ, who blessed me with the talents and abilities which resulted in this book.

I want to thank my family; my grandfather (A. D.), my parents (Bobby and Shirley, who are my best friends and my biggest supporters), my sisters (Pamela, Patricia, and Sheila), my nieces (Jasmine and Tymani), my nephews (Shaquille and Jalen), and my adopted brothers (Heath Cleaver, José A. Duarte, Ron Tiongco, and James P. Williams Jr.) for their support on all my life's endeavors. Also thanks to Amy Bittner, Hong Leng, Nori Lopez, and Rosie Tabilangan; you are more like my sisters than my friends. My family, I love you all dearly.

A special thanks to Veronica, Kevin Comer, and my college professor Teresa Hayes. Veronica was partly my inspiration for writing. Kevin and Veronica were major influences in encouraging me to publish this manuscript.

Thanks to my two vitamins; Vitamin E (Elizabeth) and Vitamin O (Oneida Taveras). Even though I lack my daily recommended dosage of these vitamins they brightened my day when I see them both and their smiles. Elizabeth has inspired me to write again after 5 years. Oneida, my best friend in Houston has been my voice of reason since she entered my life. She and her family have accepted me as part of theirs. These two women remind me each day that there are still genuinely nice people in this world.

I would like to thank my editors and proofreaders Nidia Alvarado, Tony Alvarez, Leticia Blanton, Stephanie Lopez, Sonia Morales, and Mayra Rojas. These individuals are my friends as well as my editors and proofreaders. Sonia found the first initial errors in my manuscript and has been editing my emails since our Horizon days. Leticia has shared her wisdom with me even though I'm an elder statesman by comparison to her (I'm 2 days older).

I would like to thank my dentist, Dr. Stephen S. Wolters, DDS and his dental staff. Dr. Wolters encouraged me to share the significance behind the book cover photograph.

I would like to give a special thanks to my birthday bro, David

Spellman III for taking my back cover photograph.

Also, I would like to thank my current and past friends and family that have encouraged, inspired, and contributed to make me the person whom I am. There are a lot of people I can think of, but it's impossible to list you all.

Photograph taken by
Bobby Lathan Jr., July 1997
The former Alfred P. Murrah Federal Building site
Oklahoma City, OK

Also, I would like to dedicate this book to all of GOD's angels that are watching over us.

Photograph taken by
Bobby Lathan Jr., 1990s
Paternal grandparents' house
Bienville Parish, LA

My grandfather has always been one of my major influences in my life. There is so much that I have learned from him about communication, hard work, honesty, and integrity. He is one of the men that I strive to be.

INTRODUCTION

These poems are more like stories of my life experiences and the life experiences of my family and friends. Some of them are about dreams and goals that I have had during my lifetime. My life's journey has been one of love; learning how to give it to and receive it from individuals unconditionally. This book was difficult for me to write and release, because it has been a very intimate journey in discovering me as well as other people. As I have grown as a person my writing has matured. I decided to release this to share my experiences and the experiences of others in the hope that people can learn from it and share it with others.

I hope you will enjoy reading this book as much as I had writing it. These life experiences are universal regardless of age, nationality, race, or religion. I hope when you finish reading you will walk away with a better appreciation of the people in your life. My objectives are to open up lines of communication and strengthen relationships through the realizations that the more we think and feel we are alone the more we should realize we are not, and that the more we think we are different from people the more we are alike and have in common with them.

Happy reading!

Bobby Lathan Jr.

"Seek first to understand, then to be understood"
- Stephen R. Covey

Photograph taken by
Bobby Lathan Jr., August 1979
Illinois

This photograph of my mother and my youngest sister is the first one that I remember taking. That moment in my life developed a lifelong love of photography.

HUMBLE BEGINNINGS

Photograph taken by
Bobby Lathan Jr., 1989
Bienville Parish, LA

This home is where my father grew up and his journey began. In essence these are my roots and part of my life's story. I took the photograph as my father escorted my youngest sister and myself through the home as he recalled his childhood memories.

A
LIFE'S
JOURNEY

REFLECTIONS
OF LIFE AND LOVE
THROUGH POETRY

WILL YOU BE MY WOMAN?
WRITTEN APRIL 1990

Oh how the sun glares right off your sparkling eyes

As the wind blows through your natural silk-like hair

Your beautiful smile which brightens my gray lonely day

You don't know how much you really mean to me

Will you be my woman?

Your face is beautiful as a bright rising sun

Your skin feels soft as a newly planted flower

There is no one who can replace you

That is why I want it to be you and me

That is why I want to know

Will you be my woman?

MY HEART'S DESIRE
WRITTEN MARCH 10, 1995

As I gaze into the sky
I think of a friend
I think about her
I think about me
I think about how our relationship could be

My emotions I suppress
Then my feelings I hide
From fear of rejection
Avoiding injury to my pride

My heart says "Yes!"
My mind says "No!"
If I allow my emotions to flow
I wonder could this relationship grow

As I sit beside her
I know she's the one for me
Can I convince her to be with me?

My challenge is now
As I sit right beside her
Will I be a coward?
Will I lose an opportunity for my heart's desire?

(Continued On Next Page)

I ask her my question

Will her answer be yes or no?

My GOD I just want to know

With my head in the clouds

My soul ignites on fire

Will she allow me to have my heart's desire?

To be the one in her life is my heart's desire

As her best friend

When the world seems to be at the end

Taking our time so our relationship can grow

To make it strong and unbreakable

To give her red roses so she can see

How very important she is to me

Then I would slow dance with her every night

Before having dinner by candlelight

So I can hold her so very tight

Then she will know everything is alright

When I see her inner beauty

I will feel happy and become inspired

That I can achieve all of her heart's desires

I HAVE A FRIEND
WITH CONTRIBUTIONS BY MICHAEL JILBERT
WRITTEN MARCH 10, 1995

I have a friend
When the world unnerves me
She comforts me with her compassion

I have a friend
When nothing seems to make sense
Her intelligence and wisdom
Restores my confidence

I have a friend
When I see her shyness
It blossoms through her inner beauty
Like a dozen lovely long stemmed red roses

I have a friend
Who has a smile
That brightens my life
Like a bright ray of sunshine

I have a friend
Who has all of these qualities
My darling you know it's you!

MY FEELINGS I HIDE
WRITTEN MARCH 11, 1995

My feelings I hide

Buried so deep inside

Not willing to love

Due to the pain of rejection within

Walking alone through the streets of life

My feelings I hide

So deep inside

With feelings of loneliness

Not willing to love

Avoiding the feelings of hurt

My feelings I hide

Since I am always alone

Not willing to love

Not allowing a broken heart to be my home

ANGEL IN THE SKY
WRITTEN MARCH 11, 1995

The stars are shining so bright
Is my angel here tonight?
Is she out there in the sky?
I wonder and I look to see
Is she the comet that just passed me?

Beautiful angel I admire and see
Will she set my soul free?
She seems so distant and far from me
I wonder if she will ever come close to me

Her hair is like silk
Her skin is like gold
I cannot believe her beauty
The heavens can hold

Her gorgeous face I see through the night
As it shines through like a heavenly light
Revealing her beauty, her wisdom, and my peace of mind
Maybe one day this heavenly angel will be mine

WHAT IS HAPPINESS?
WRITTEN MARCH 13, 1995

Why I cannot control my feelings?

Happiness has always avoided me

Happiness does not want to be a part of me

Why do I pursue it so eagerly?

Maybe happiness is so close to me

That I am just not able to see

Loneliness is my happiness

Because of no pain or fear

I just have to realize

That my loneliness will always be here

IF MY LIFE WAS ONE MOMENT
WRITTEN MARCH 16, 1995

If my life was one moment
I would spend it with you
Giving you my time
For just simply being you

If my life was one moment
I would spend it with you
Walking barefooted in the grass
Moistened by the morning dew

If my life was one moment
I would cherish it with you
In our garden planting red roses
While our love blossoms and blooms

If my life was one moment
I would spend it with you
Taking horse carriage rides
In the late afternoon

If my life was one moment
I would spend it with you
Cuddled by a fireplace
Just me with you

(Continued On Next Page)

If my life was one moment
I would spend it with you
Watching a radiant sunset
Sparkling off Lake Michigan too

If my life was one moment
I would lasso the moon
For our dinners by candlelight
At an ocean-side view

If my life was one moment
I would express my gratitude
That GOD blessed me
With a heavenly angel like you

If my life was one moment
I would spend it with you
To whisper you sweet phrases
Like, "I Love You!"

If my life was one moment
I would spend it with you
Holding hands with my inspiration
To make our dreams come true

TEARDROPS FROM THE SKY
WRITTEN MARCH 18, 1995

Teardrops from the sky

Fall for me

Because of the love that has ended

Before it has even began

Teardrops from the sky

Fall for me

Because I refuse to breakdown and cry

For hurt feelings I hide

Teardrops from the sky

Fall for me

For the sorrow in my life

Revealing the loneliness of mine

Teardrops from the sky

Fall for me

Washing away the pain in my heart

To restore my kindness, gentleness, and pride

Teardrops from the sky

Fall for me

For my soul has been restored

Concealing the love I will give no more

PLEDGING OF A HEART
WRITTEN AUGUST 25, 1995

I come to you on this mystical night

Pledging my love so special and true

Down on one knee

Giving my pure tender heart to you

Making a symbolic stand

As I elevate my commitment this night

Woman, you should understand

That you are needed in my life

So I am asking you this night

Will you be my wife?

A SEARCH FOR LOVE
WRITTEN OCTOBER 24, 1995

My soul is bruised

My ego is crushed

In pursuit of an emotion called love

What am I missing?

I do not know

It does not seem so clear

Is it because love is so close and near?

COMFORT

WRITTEN OCTOBER 24, 1995

Space is an empty place

Where the lonely souls reside

Like the distant sun

Along with the bright shining stars above

They stand alone

Attempting to comfort each other

Through a ball of spectacular light

MY GODDESS OF LOVE
WRITTEN OCTOBER 24, 1995

It was like seeing a heavenly sight
As my eyes came across her presence
My heart began to fall
Like a shooting star from the sky
Blazing a trail of spectacular fire

Her warmth glows like a radiant sunset
That sparkles from her precious gemstone eyes
The softness of her skin is like a red rose petal
Her clouds of shyness hints of her inner beauty

While her spirit soars through the sky
Like a precious white dove
Her qualities are very rare
Hidden only to the naked eye
Could she be my goddess of love in disguise?

SPARK OF A HEART
WRITTEN OCTOBER 24, 1995

When I first saw her
It ignited a spark
In a place deep down in my heart

Beginning an accumulation of a mountain of fire
Filling my soul with passion and desire
What is this feeling I have inside of me?
Could it be my heart is in love?

WHY DO I LOVE THEE?
WRITTEN OCTOBER 25, 1995

Why do I love thee?
Could it be how the wind blows
Through her silky black hair?
Or is it her tranquil eyes?
Reminding me of a crystal blue sky

Why do I love thee?
I really would like to know
Is it the warmth of her smile?
That brightens my day like a golden sunrise
Or is it her mysterious mist of shyness?
She hides behind

Why do I love thee?
GOD, please tell me so
Is it her precious heart?
That sparkles like a diamond

Photograph taken by
Bobby Lathan Jr., January 1997
Lake Michigan
near Chicago, IL

This photograph is one of my favorites. It's a sunrise over Lake Michigan around 7 in the morning.

AN IMPORTANT EMOTION
WRITTEN JUNE 2, 1997

An important emotion is love
That enlightens everyone's day
It brings devastation
In the midst of celebration
It brings encouragement
In the midst of hopelessness

Like an author to a mystery novel
Uncertainty is provided by love
As the end of the chapter furnishes suspense
With suspicion into a new beginning

Love restores wounded souls
Igniting a raging fire of forgiveness
Rising like a radiant sunrise
Healing shallow empty voids
Blacken like a dark wilderness cave

Love disrupts life with ups and downs
Like a predestined emotional roller coaster
Fulfilling our restless spirits with an eternal ecstasy
As well as a momentary hardship and pain

(Continued On Next Page)

Then love cultivates a compassionate spirit
As gentle as a summer breeze
Skipping across a wave
Of the tranquil blue ocean

As like a mother nursing her young
Love allows you to mature and grow
It is what makes life worth living
Motivating everyone to keep going on

CAN LOVE TRANSCEND TIME?

WRITTEN MAY 23, 1998

She Says:
You waited too long
We've been distanced by time
How can you say you love me?
Your heart is no longer a part of mine
Love can't transcend time

I haven't seen you for months
Then the months added up into years
Missing out on sharing your laughter
Allowing you to comfort my tears
Love can't transcend time

Why do you ignore me and refuse to hear?
What can I say to make it really clear?
Love just can't transcend time

He Responds:
Yes, love transcends time
For years I've been giving you mine
I love you stronger now
Than I loved you then
Why should you let time separate us again?

Yes, love transcends time
I feel it in my heart and mind
Reminiscing over experiences we've shared
Binding us in love no one can compare
Why are you so willing to just deny?

Yes, love transcends time
How come?
Our love resides inside our hearts
Only your denial is keeping us apart

CAN LOVE TRANSCEND TIME?
REVISED BY JOSÉ A. DUARTE
REVISED MAY 28, 1998

She Says:

> You waited too long
> We've been distanced by time
> How can you say you love me?
> Your heart is no longer a part of mine
> Love can't transcend time

He Responds:

> Yes, love transcends time
> For years I've been giving you mine
> I love you stronger now
> Than I loved you then
> Why should you let time separate us again?

She Answers:

> I haven't seen you for months
> Then the months added up into years
> Missing out on sharing your laughter
> Allowing you to comfort my tears
> Love can't transcend time

He Replies:

> Yes, love transcends time
> I feel it in my heart and mind
> Reminiscing over experiences we've shared
> Binding us in love no one can compare
> Why are you so willing to just deny?

She Rebuts:

> Why do you ignore me and refuse to hear?
> What can I say to make it really clear?
> Love just can't transcend time

He Says:

> Yes, love transcends time
> How come?
> Our love resides inside our hearts
> Only your denial is keeping us apart

Photograph taken by
Aida Alba, June 1998
Chicago, IL

One of the happiest moments of my life was when I received my Bachelor of Science Degree. This has been one of my life's greatest accomplishments. It was a struggle to meet that goal, because during that time in my life I had been working a full-time job and going to school full-time. Working full-time while acquiring my degree was a blessing. I learned many valuable lessons from my factory experience. My experiences taught me about not making assumptions about people and situations. I have learned the difference between situations and concepts. I realized that it was very important to learn various concepts from all situations. Learning that lesson has helped me resolve most situations in my

Photograph taken by
Aida Alba, June 1998
Chicago, IL

life, because it has given me the perspective that solutions are not situation specific. If you understand a concept or an idea it will help solve any problem or circumstance that enters your life.

Here I am sharing my moment of great accomplishment with my parents, who taught me the valuable lesson of communication. It has helped me to grow and strengthen my relationships with my family and friends. Through them and their guidance I am a more loving and compassionate person.

LOVE WAS NOT ENOUGH

WRITTEN APRIL 17, 1999

Love was not enough
It took me some time
To realize I had your heart
But it's no longer mine

Love was not enough
Because I did not know
When I was pursuing my dreams
Being with you was one of them

Love was not enough
To get us through the tears
Even though you decided to move on
I still missed you all these years

Love was not enough
How could I be a fool?
Now I must experience life
Knowing I will always love you

ANGRY WITH ME

WRITTEN MAY 28, 1999

It wasn't my fault

I have known that for years

You did this to me!

But why is the only anger

Is the anger I feel for me?

Why did I give you control?

So much control over me

Causing severe damage to my self-esteem

You caused me to resist

People's attempts of intimacy

While rejecting their love for me

I nearly ruined my life

Because of what you did to me

I guess that's why I can't blame you

And I am so angry with me

Photograph taken by
Bobby Lathan Jr., June 1999
Book Cover Photograph
Bienville Parish, LA

I was blessed to have all of my grandparents living until I was 27. My paternal grandmother passed away in June 1999, after her funeral I decided to walk from the cemetery to my grandfather's house. During my walk I took this picture with more awareness of my mortality. Looking back it was a transitional moment, in a symbolic way I believe I walked into manhood that day.

WHY DID MY LONELINESS COME HERE?
WRITTEN JANUARY 1, 2000

During the New Year's jubilation
My eyes glazed with tears
As I watched couples bring in
The new millennium
The new century
The new year

As I stood wondering
Why did my loneliness come here?
Could it be also I'm thinking
Why love has been so elusive in my prior years?

Or is it a longing for the experience
Of obtaining true love once in my life
The type of love when you gaze
Into someone's eyes for the first time
Knowing that your feelings are mutual and everlasting

Came And Gone Again
Written May 30, 2000

How could I let it happen again?
After my experiences throughout the years
What I am looking for
Is one of GOD's earthly angels

When I first placed my eyes upon her
My feelings were of disbelief
I gently took her hand
As I approached her to dance
A nervous sentiment accumulated within that night
When I held her in my arms

With awareness she had captured my heart
As I gazed into her eyes
Due to my apprehension
Inside I held back my infatuation

That moment seemed like an eternity
As time slithered away
I began to loosen my embrace
From around her waist
Realizing my opportunity had came and gone again

REDEMPTION?
WRITTEN MAY 30, 2000

Staring outside onto the street

I watched people passing by

With thoughts dancing through their heads

While I juggle with thoughts of mine

My thoughts are about my recently missed opportunity

The opportunity to have an angel in my life

Searching if there is a possibility of redemption

To reveal my heart

What could I do to find her?

If I locate her

Will I capture hers?

Anxiety and excitement has come over me

As I embark on my mission of uncertainty

To take a stand

As I overcome my fear

To express the fascination

I have for her

DID I COMMIT A CRIME?

WRITTEN JUNE 4, 2000

How can you say I am wrong?

For feeling this way

Why did you turn your back on me?

For a single statement I made

We use to be close friends

But it has changed in such a short time

Now that you look at me

Like I committed a crime

All I did was tell you what I felt

And how you impacted my life

LAUGHTER
WRITTEN JUNE 4, 2000

Laughter is the medicine
That heals all your ills

It lifts you up
When you are down

It warms your spirit
When something gives you the chills

DREAMS
WRITTEN JUNE 4, 2000

As a child I would dream

About all the experiences

Life would bring to me

Obstacles will come into our way

It makes the steps

To obtaining our dreams

Worthwhile each day

EMPTINESS OF MINE
WRITTEN JUNE 4, 2000

My spirit feels so vacant

Having me ponder why?

I just feel so lonely

Unwanted

Not loved

But why?

I've always been searching

Never really asking for much

Just to love

Be loved

Fulfilling this emptiness of mine

REMEMBER
WRITTEN JUNE 4, 2000

I remember when you first caught my eye
Revealing my mixed emotions buried deep inside
You are the most beautiful woman to me
But I just can't let my emotions run free

I know we are friends
I want to be close
Because you are the woman
That I care for the most

You are like a single yellow rose
That stands apart
That's why I pray to GOD
I will win your heart

THE IMPORTANT THINGS IN LIFE
WRITTEN JUNE 4, 2000

Sometimes we get caught in life's events

Forgetting what is important

The people who influence our lives

The family members whom always have been there

The friendships that we have made

Through the good and bad times

The loved ones who support us

TIME IS A PRECIOUS THING
WRITTEN JUNE 4, 2000

Time is a precious thing
That we receive everyday
We should be careful
Not to let it waste away

We can't recapture the past
Nor can we expect a future
So cherish the time we have today
Before your opportunity fades away

THE OPPORTUNITY HAS COME AGAIN
WRITTEN JUNE 19, 2000

Darkness covered the sky that night
As the angel and I began strolling down the sidewalk
At last, the moment I had been anticipating arrived

In that instant, months of enthusiasm and anxiety
Had climaxed into minutes
Of revealing the thoughts of my heart
With shyness illuminating from my spirit

As the curiosity of my mind
Exclaimed for fulfillment
I expressed my desire
That I wanted to know her better
To resolve the question
Why has she captured my heart?

Her eyes began to widen with amazement
As she glanced into my soul
Tranquilly she smiled with an attempt
To conceal her gently blushing face

Will she appreciate my openness and honesty?
Only time will tell
As I must step back
To wait and see

NEEDS NOT TO REMAIN
WRITTEN JUNE 22, 2000

Why is there so much pain inside my heart?
For years I have been seeking someone
Just to love and to be with me

Why is it so easy for me to love?
Why it so hard for people to love me?
What am I doing wrong?
Why does everyone leave me?

My life has not been easy
GOD, please remove all of my pain
I no longer deserve it
In here it needs not to remain

AGONY OF THE HEART

WRITTEN JUNE 22, 2000

Lord, I do not understand

The agony of my heart

Why do we struggle to get through life?

Seeking an objective so obtainable

But elusive

That we will stare at it in the face

Unable to embrace

While our fears makes us cling to an illusion

FRUSTRATION
WRITTEN JULY 3, 2000

Why has frustration hit me so hard?

What is it that I feel I have lost?

Is it my desire?

To Love?

To Live?

To Learn?

Or is it conflict?

The conflict that is brewing deep within

My spirit has realized the time for change has come

But the mind wants to remain the same

I know I cannot go on

Living my life this way

Right now I really do not know what to do

I know the answers to my questions are all inside of me

FRIENDSHIP
Written November 21, 2000

I remember the day we met like it was yesterday

Your first words from our initial chat

Still echo in my head as if you said them today

I want you to know those words mean a lot to me

Even through the years of getting to know each other

As we have laughed and cried together

Experiencing life's moments of joy and pain

We have watched each other grow as individuals

At times, I know I have taken you for granted

Attempting to overcompensate for it later

I want to thank you for making me see

That striving to be simplistic

Will bring out the best part of me

You made me realize I do not need to do anything

Except for to be the better person I want to be

You have made changes to your life and words cannot express

How very proud I am of your accomplishments

I never expected that our casual conversation

Would affect my life this way

It has blossomed into the special friendship we have today

Looking forward to the future years to come

I will love you always and thank you for being my friend

TIME STANDS STILL
WRITTEN DECEMBER 31, 2000

The days seems to dash by
As time stands still
The moment is nearing
For my next encounter with the angel

Eagerness has come over me
As I prepare for our interaction
My thoughts are inquisitive about my manners
How they will open her heart to me?

A heart that appears to be cautious to any connection
What could have made it so wary of opening up to others?
Will my confident spirit conquer any obstacles to her heart?

The answers I have envisioned
In my heart as well as my mind
As she will see the caring
I have for her in my soul
With my openness, honesty, and dedication
Will I accomplish my goal?

LOVE KNOWS NO DISTANCE
WRITTEN FEBRUARY 17, 2002

My words are hard to come by
When I have thoughts of you
It's like I am living a dream
Since the day I met you

It started with a casual conversation
With thoughts of friendship from the start
But I don't know what has happened
Because you have connected with my heart

Even though we are separated by distance
As an effect we also are by time
Still love knows no distance
If it stands the test of time

NEVER SEEN NEVER HEARD
WRITTEN MARCH 27, 2002

Starting life ambitious I searched
For materialistic things and goals
That most people achieved and received

Through all of my struggles in life
During my triumphs and failures
Something was always missing

A face I have never seen
A voice I have never heard
A person to share my life with
A person to share my love

FIRST MEETING
WRITTEN APRIL 8, 2002

As I walked by you caught my eye

Then I noticed you glanced my way

You smiled at me and I reciprocated

Your personality warmth radiated

An intriguing essence that I have never seen

It draws me towards you

Then without a clue you are standing before me

I ask you your name and you do the same

We talk for awhile as we both smile

For a few minutes that seemed like an eternity

Time had escaped and now we must part

As we both agree it was a pleasure to meet each other

I ask for your phone number

You say call me anytime

Then we both thank each other for a great time

Photograph taken by
Bobby Lathan Jr., June 2002
Field of Dreams Movie Site
Dyersville, IA

I visited this site during another transitional period in my life. I grew into independence during that time. I had been laid off from a job and I decided to pick up and move from Illinois to Texas with no prospects and my strong faith that everything would be alright. Now I have been living in Texas for almost 7 years.

A New Beginning
Written July 23, 2002

With my back turned on the past

I walk facing towards the future

Things and people seem no longer familiar

Because they no longer exist

Or they have changed

Heading to my uncertain future

With eyes opened to endless possibilities

ONCE AGAIN
WRITTEN JULY 23, 2002

It has happened to me again
Just hanging with someone as a friend
I do not know what came over me

As I opened my eyes then I see
She has really meant more to me
Once more I must let go again
Because she can only be my friend

LETTING GO

WRITTEN JULY 24, 2002

Why must I go through this again?

Seeing something that I thought could be real

But it is really a dream turned into an illusion

Why must I hold on to a dream?

A dream that has eluded me all my life

A dream that has brought nothing but pain

It is time for me to move on

It is time for me to let go

A MOMENT IN TIME
WRITTEN JULY 25, 2002

Time after time
I have written about angels
In my poetry and in my journal

I never believed
I would ever see or even meet one
But GOD has blessed me with one
Since the day I have met you

I do not know how much time
We have left to spend together
But if we ever part ways
I will not cry or be sad
I will rejoice and be happy

That I have had an angel
For one gleaming moment
That has touched my life

In my heart a part of your angelic spirit
I will always carry with me
Something that has changed me
For the better and forever

NEVER LOVE AGAIN
WRITTEN JULY 30, 2002

How can I have so much love to give?
But can only share a fraction of my love

Time and time again
I have feelings of frustration mixed with love
Sometimes I think life would be more meaningful
If I was unable to love

I would avoid all the heartache
I would not experience any pain
I would be able to look into a woman's eyes
Knowing that I would never feel anything again

CROSSROADS
WRITTEN AUGUST 9, 2002

We started our journeys through life
On our separate paths
Never knowing our two paths would cross

I did not expect a casual meeting
To blossom into a loving friendship
Nor did I expect my heart to fall in love

As you struggle with your past
To develop your future
As I look at you as our future

With our desires heading on separate paths
We struggle with our hearts in turmoil
To hold on to what we have today

GOD'S BLESSING TO ME
WRITTEN AUGUST 11, 2002

Why have I been searching
For something so near to me
The love of GOD inside of me

GOD, YOU have blessed me
With a wonderful life
An excellent family
A loving heart

It took me so long to realize
What I seek has been always hidden in me

DECISIONS OF A HEART IN TURMOIL
WRITTEN AUGUST 12, 2002

My heart is in turmoil
There is no wondering why
I am in agony over saying goodbye

Things happened so fast
That I could not see
That what I was looking for
Was right next to me

You went back to your past
In hopes of a brighter future
While you are shutting me out
To prevent our love from nurturing

As you can see I am in a difficult position
Dealing with the pain of our separation
My feelings are in turmoil inside of me
Because I know that you still care for me

Should I let you go?
So my hurt will go
Or should I keep fighting?
So our love can grow

HOW CAN I MOVE ON?
WRITTEN AUGUST 12, 2002

How can I move on?

Knowing that every corner I turned down

When I see another woman

I see not her

But you

My thoughts are not of her

But they are of thoughts of you

When I hear another woman's voice

I hear sounds of you

When I smell the scent of another woman

It reminds me of the scent of you

When I look into another woman's eyes

I do not see beauty in her

It reminds me of the beauty

I found in you

How can I move on?

When I am reminded

Of what made me

Fall in love with you

TO MY WIFE WITH LOVE

WRITTEN AUGUST 18, 2002

For years I have been seeking you

But I have not yet found you

Or maybe I have

And I do not know

Or maybe I have

I know it

And you do not

Today I reaffirm my commitment

To conclude my search

Wherever I must go

I will

Whatever I must do

I will

To find you and to share with you

The respect, honesty, and commitment

To the love that we both deserve during our lifetimes

MEMORY OF YOU
WRITTEN AUGUST 18, 2002

As I knelt by your side
Then I began to reveal to you
The secrets of my heart

My feelings of love for you
As I peered into your eyes
During the revelation of my soul

Slowly I began to scan
Every feature of your face
Your silky brown-blonde hair
Neatly held combed back into a pony tail

Your beautiful brown eyes that shine brightly
As your soft round glowing cheeks are lifted high
By your smile that enlightens any room you enter
Then your alluring lips
That I have only kissed gently in my dreams

I memorized your features
As if it was the first time
Realizing I have always seen them
But never in this way before
Praying that it will not be the last time
I would ever see such beauty during my lifetime

YOUR BEAUTY IS YOUR SOUL

WRITTEN AUGUST 18, 2002

Before I fell in love
With the beauty of your face
I fell in love
With the beauty of your soul

Since I have met you
I have watched you
Express your love to your family
Wishing that someday that I would be able
To share that experience with you

Knowing that when the beauty
Of other women fades
Yours will remain
Because yours is not just of the body
Your beauty is the extension of your soul

MY ENDLESS ENDEAVOR
WRITTEN AUGUST 18, 2002

Continuing on my endeavor

As my weary heart heals

To seek what I desire and deserve

I must move pass

The pain of the past

In order to achieve

My hopes in the future

EXTRAORDINARY
WRITTEN AUGUST 19, 2002

You are an extraordinary woman
Who has lived an extraordinary life
Dealing with so much difficulty and pain
Early during your young life

Within a month you have touched my life
Changing my perceptions
As well as altering my life's direction

THE EASIEST THING
WRITTEN AUGUST 19, 2002

Loving you is the easiest thing I can do

Or for that fact any man can do

But why did I make it so hard?

When the radiance of your personality

Slithered by the defenses of my spirit

Even infiltrating pass the guards of my heart

The essence of your spirit

Beckons everyone around you

For someone just spending a little time with you

For someone just sheltering you

From the storms of life and to protect you

And for someone simply just to love you

WHY DO I LOVE YOU?
WRITTEN AUGUST 19, 2002

Why do I love you?
Well let me tell you a few things
That caused these feelings of mine

During all of our intriguing talks
You ask me about my ordinary days
Before I go to sleep at night
Sweet dreams you wish for me to guide my way

Then every time I see you
After a long and trying day
I know that I will see your angelic smile
That will brighten the rest of my day

After seeing you with your sister
Cuddling with her in a loving way
Then at that point I knew
You are a very special person
In an unique and compassionate way

Of all the people I have known
During the span of my life
You are the one that I have prayed for
To be my best friend, my lover, and my wife

CLOUDS OF ILLUSIONS
WRITTEN AUGUST 19, 2002

Why are these feelings consuming me?

It is because I never experience true love

Even once during my life

That these feelings of ecstasy

Are just clouds of illusions

Just hiding the truth

That my lonely empty spirit

Is desperately holding onto an illusion

To keep the love burning inside my heart alive

WHY SHOULD I HOLD ON?
WRITTEN AUGUST 19, 2002

Why should I hold on?
To the feelings within me
Knowing I am being selfish
Because your feelings of love are not for me
You told me I would be a good friend
To just hang out with and to be around

Why should I hold on?
Knowing that this cannot last for long
I know I desire a future for us
To hold on to this dream
Would cause us nothing but pain

It is time for me to move on
Because of the emotions in my heart
I love you now and always
Knowing this love will never depart

MY DESIRES

WRITTEN AUGUST 19, 2002

So much love I carry

In this lonely world with me

Why has it been so hard?

To share these passions inside me

What are my desires?

To be able to see in a woman's eyes

All the affection she has for me

To feel her gentle caressing touch

To have her convey

Her emotions for me

To feel a yearning all day

For the tender kiss of her lips

Then cuddling next to her sexy body

So she can appreciate

That I will always be there for her

To protect her for the rest of our lives

As we lead into our passionate night

Expressing our love until the early morning light

I Need YOUR Guidance

Written August 21, 2002

Lord I need your guidance

I am lost and do not know which path to take

Why am I seeking the approval of people?

Instead of seeking approval from YOU

My heart is hurting so bad

I know through YOU

You will take away the pain

So why am I not willing

To give the situation to YOU?

MY DAILY PRAYER
WRITTEN AUGUST 21, 2002

Lord I believe and trust in YOU

To guide me on my way

To give me the courage to go on

To follow YOU for the rest of my days

I know the storms of life

Will invade my sunny days

Give me the strength to go on

That is my daily prayer

LOVING ME IS THE SAME
WRITTEN AUGUST 21, 2002

GOD, why do I go through this experience?

Which happens to me over and over again?

A woman that I fell in love with

Instead of being with me

She chooses another man

MY Son, loving ME is the same

Loving ME will take away the pain

Before you can love her

You have to love ME

This is the lesson I want you to see

But GOD why don't YOU listen to me?

Why doesn't she love me?

This experience is too much to bear

Sometimes I wonder why I even care

MY Son, loving ME is the same

This has never changed

I've listened to you but you haven't listened to ME

Your love for her shouldn't come before ME

(Continued On Next Page)

But GOD my heart hurts so much
The pain seems to never end
So Lord why don't you close my heart?
So I will never love again

MY Son, loving ME is the same
Why must I repeat this again and again?
I can't close your heart
Because I want you to see
That the love that is coming from you
Is the love generated from ME!

But GOD I just don't understand
I know I'm a decent man
What could be wrong with me?
Why does it seem no one is willing to love me?

MY Son, loving ME is the same
I will never leave in the end
I will always love you
You just need to love ME
MY LOVE WILL SUPPLY ALL OF YOUR NEEDS!

MY CONTINUED PLIGHT
WRITTEN AUGUST 23, 2002

I did it again!

I can't believe it!

This beautiful woman has done something to me

Walking into a store I just stopped and stared

I'm surprised, she didn't notice my glare

My heart said to me, "It doesn't hurt to try!"

In pursuit of the love that my past has denied

In that moment my heart does a good deed

Will she see this is a sincere part of me?

Impressed by her character that she had shared

As she thanked me and said the words I have always dread

Hearing these words were very discouraging to my plight

As she said to me, "I have someone in my life"

Now I must move on to continue my search

To find my special someone somewhere on this Earth

SAYING GOODBYE
WRITTEN AUGUST 23, 2002

Saying goodbye is the hardest thing to do

Even when it is dealing with someone special as you

We sometimes ignore things in our paths

Because we are desperately holding onto things of the past

Even in the pursuit of reaching our destined future

We tend to hold onto things to keep us from being nurtured

Realizing that we have great emotion and a desire to grow

We know we must move on and it is time to let go

IN A SHORT TIME
WRITTEN OCTOBER 1, 2002

Why have these feelings come over me?

For a woman whom I have never seen

She speaks with wisdom beyond her years

That radiates her compassionate spirit

Bringing the strongest man to tears

As she is just simply being the best person she can be

Her character and compassion fascinates me

I have only known her for a short time

That is why her character has blown my mind

That is why I cannot control these emotions of mine

Photograph taken by
Bobby Lathan Jr., November 2002
Maternal grandparents' house
Alexandria, LA

This photograph of my father was taken for my maternal grandmother's funeral. It was a difficult transitional life moment, because I was creating a new life in a new place and my grandmother's death was unexpected and devastating to me. That experience affected me greatly. I was unable to express myself in writing for more than a year. After writing the poem, *"Time To Say Goodbye"* it took me almost 5 years to start writing again.

DEDICATIONS
FOR
TIME TO SAY GOODBYE

LUCILLE HAMPTON GOODMAN
JANUARY 24, 1920 – OCTOBER 26, 2002

HAZEL LATHAN
JULY 9, 1921 - JUNE 9, 1999

MURPHY GOODMAN JR.
JANUARY 28, 1917 – MAY 23, 2006

MY GRANDPARENTS

I MISS YOU
I WILL NEVER FORGET YOU
AND
I WILL ALWAYS LOVE YOU!

TIME TO SAY GOODBYE
WRITTEN MARCH 24, 2004

How can I say goodbye

Since you went away

My tears have been falling

Since that very day

I have been hoping

You would return

For a very long time

But it is time to let go

To begin healing this pain of mine

I know it will be very hard

To never see you again

But it comforts me to know

Your love for me will never end!

READY TO SHARE MY HEART

WRITTEN JANUARY 19, 2009

Walking through the hall

I was ready to pass you by

I took one quick look

Then your eyes connected to mine

As I stepped past you

Then you said to me

Could you come over to speak with me?

I said to you

Not right now I have some place to be

As I stopped dead in my tracks

I just waited to see

My mind was wondering

What does this woman want with me?

She said to me

I know it has been quite awhile

Since you got me to laugh

And you've seen my smile

Let's move beyond the past

To make a new start

Because I'm ready now

To share my heart

SHADOWS OF DARKNESS
WRITTEN FEBRUARY 13, 2009

No longer any passion

Void of any pain

As shadows of darkness

Creeps through the walls of a heart

Once filled with warmth and love

But slowly it tapered away

The light has expired

Bitterness has triumphed

Now coldness resides

For the soul no longer remains

A NEW START

WRITTEN FEBRUARY 13, 2009

Looking into your eyes
All I could see was a passion
Burning deep inside of me

I want to pursue the love
That I feel inside of me
But I was afraid of you rejecting me

As I hear your words
I feel relief and surprise
When you said to me
That I have caught your eye

With the revelations of our hearts
We prepare our lives for our new start

ANTICIPATION
WRITTEN FEBRUARY 13, 2009

My heart trembles with anticipation

As I prepare to see

The woman that fascinates me

I like her

Does she like me?

Has my heart revealed

It's secret for her to see?

Will our interaction give me a clue?

Could this be a beginning of something new?

FEELINGS OF MINE
WRITTEN FEBRUARY 13, 2009

She treats me unfairly
As well as unkind
In an attempt to deter
These feelings of mine

She doesn't understand
I would accept her as a friend
But she treats me
Like every other man

She really wants to ask
What did I do to make you feel this way?
That's a good question
Here's what I would say

Through our simple interaction
She has captured my heart
With her hints of shyness
Is where I will start

Also she's very soft spoken
That's another part
Then her natural beauty
Gives you a true sense of her heart

(Continued On Next Page)

As we move on to her sense of humor

Now that's the funny part

With the love for her family

She has impressed me from the start

As I concluded

The revelations of my heart

Oh did I mention?

Also she's smart!

She shows off her beauty

In these simple ways

If I was standing before her

That's what I would say

Photograph taken by
David Spellman III, March 2009
Houston, TX

Ok, this is me just being me. David wanted me to fix my hair for the back cover picture and I'm just too accommodating. During this moment, I was finalizing completing my first book as a published author.

INSPIRATION
WRITTEN MARCH 19, 2009

Inspiration is a word
That means so much to me
As I stand here before you
With you standing right next to me

Still I cannot believe it
I have reached this moment in my life
As we both prepare to unite our lives

You have expanded my purpose
You have brought love into my life
Now that we are together as husband and wife

THANKS FOR READING!
LIVE! LAUGH! LOVE!

"A day without laughter is a day wasted"
- Charlie Chaplin

CPSIA information can be obtained
at www.ICGtesting.com
Printed in the USA
BVHW041155291218
536686BV00003B/158/P

9 780578 007311